Praise for *The Self-Worth Solution*

"Wow! Eye-Opening and Highly Recommended!"

"Wow! The information Holly has packed into this book is fantastic! Actionable, eye-opening concepts about self-sabotage that hit you right between the eyes, backed up with real-life examples and solutions. Her writing not only conveys such truth (the kind you might not even want to hear), but in such a conversational, "Hey, I'm right here with you" way that made me feel like I was sitting at her kitchen counter sharing a cup of coffee. Holly knows her stuff and is definitely one to have on your side when it comes to anything in the area of self-worth. After all, without self-worth (and Holly's expert guidance) we can't shine our brilliance in the world the way we are each uniquely designed to do. Highly recommended!"

Pamela Zimmer
Author, Speaker, Mentor
www.PamelaZimmer.com

"A Masterpiece"

"*The Self-Worth Solution* is a Masterpiece. Holly's book is a work of art for women. Authentic, gutsy, and full of real stories. She covers the important topics of shame and grief along with sharing with us the tools to recover our self-worth. Grab a copy for you, and another for a friend, sister, mentee or daughter!"

Diane Cunningham, M.Ed.
Founder and President
National Association of Christian Women
Entrepreneurs
www.nacwe.org

"Finally a Book That Offers Answers!"

"*The Self-Worth Solution* is an eye-opening journey through self-awareness. Finally a book that offers answers to resolve the self-sabotage that plagues so many strong women. We DESERVE success, and this book will help us achieve it!"

Cherise Natschke
Freelance Photographer

"Incredibly Helpful"

"In her book, *The Self-Worth Solution*, Holly's perspective on self-worth and self-esteem was incredibly helpful in opening my eyes to destructive, self-sabotaging behaviors I was living in my life and business. This topic is for the brave soul who truly values growth and improvement, because without addressing these deeply rooted issues, you will continue to be debilitated by the stumbling blocks of ignorance, denial or maybe even worse – the paralyzing fear of greater success. By recognizing damaging thought patterns, addressing the root causes, and suggesting practical cures, Holly proves that anyone – both entrepreneur and employee alike – can realize their potential and purpose in life. I definitely recommend that everyone take the time to read this book!

Morgan Waggoner
www.WaggonerWellness.com

"Engaging and Inspiring"

"The Self-Worth Solution empathetically addresses the basic issues of flawed self-concept that are too common in the female population today. Her transparency about her own journey to reclaim her own self-worth is engaging and inspiring, because most people are more inspired by those who fall and learn to pick themselves up than by those who appear to have it all together. The advice and tips Holly Doherty presents are not complicated and very practical... a succinct and easy read with a positive and useful message."

Ruth Lucas, MPsy
Professional Consultant, Life Coach and Author
www.LucasSeminars.com

The Self-Worth Solution for Smart Entrepreneurs

Know Your Self-Worth,
Grow Your Net Worth

Holly Doherty

www.HollyDoherty.com

$\mathscr{P}^3$

$\mathscr{P}$lum $\mathscr{P}$ickle $\mathscr{P}$ress

Copyright Notice

First Printing, 2016

ISBN-13: 978-0692681244

ISBN-10: 0692681248

Printed in the United States of America

Contents

Introduction

Self-esteem is a hot topic these days. Schools are talking about it. Anti-bullying campaigns are built around it. Even some retail giants are jumping on the bandwagon.

A few years ago, Dove® launched a series of ads called the Campaign For Real Beauty. It's a movement designed to combat the onslaught of unrealistic, unattainable beauty standards that women face every day, by celebrating the beauty of every-day women. Women with wrinkles. Women with curves. Women with real-looking bodies. They based this campaign on a global study that found that only 2% of women worldwide would consider themselves beautiful, and that anxiety over feeling beautiful contributes to low self-esteem at a very early age. In fact, those pressures increase with age, and self-esteem plummets accordingly.

Can you relate? I know I can.

I struggled with low self-esteem and feeling unworthy most of my life - not just because I didn't feel beautiful, but because I felt unlovable and worthless. I was emotionally and sexually abused for almost 20 years of my life. The final episode was a 5 year marriage to a man who was physically and emotionally abusive. I wasn't allowed to make any real decisions without him. Even my clothes had to meet his approval. I'd spend 20 minutes standing in the peanut butter aisle, debating whether to get the 8 oz jar or the 12 oz one, because the consequences of making the wrong decision were devastating. By the time that marriage ended, I was an empty shell of the person I used to be. I had zero self-esteem and didn't even know who I was anymore.

I compensated for my low self-esteem my entire life by being an over-achiever, thinking that I could *earn* my worth by doing enough. Well, if you've ever tried to do that, you know that it doesn't work. Not in the long run. Because after every A grade, after every award I earned or competition I won, I was left with me, laying on my bed at night still feeling crappy about myself, and looking for the next achievement to help me feel worthy. It was a never ending cycle, because I was looking for external validation – someone to tell me I was worthy - rather than looking inside myself to find my worth.

My lack of self-worth really held me back from pursuing my dreams also. As long as I can remember, I wanted to be a writer. Instead, I ended up in a physical therapy career. I found it very rewarding, but I went that direction mostly because I didn't have enough faith in myself to pursue my life-long dream of being a writer.

No one would have known by looking at me that I didn't believe in myself. I had a great life on the outside: a Master's degree from one of the most competitive Physical Therapy schools in the country, a well-paying career, good friends. But my low self-esteem kept me a prisoner to doubt, fear, and guilt. I'd second guess my decisions. I gave up my dreams because I thought, "Who am I to dream this big? Who am I to think that *I* can accomplish all this? What makes me think I can pull that off – or that I even deserve it?"

Quite honestly, my low self-esteem kept me from fulfilling the purpose I was made for.

It took me decades to repair my shattered self-esteem – countless hours of therapy, hundreds of books, and lots of trial and error until I put together a system that really works.

I talk about it openly now because I realize that silence – based on shame and fear of rejection – keeps these wounds from

> *Secrecy breeds shame. But when you're open about your struggles, you realize you're not alone, and you can begin to heal.*

healing. Secrecy breeds shame, and it becomes a self-perpetuating cycle. But when you're open about your struggles, when you bring them to light in a safe environment, you realize you're not alone and you can begin to heal.

And you're not alone. So many women I talk to – women I mentor and coach – express the same doubts, the same fears, the same insecurities. The details of their stories are unique, but the results are the same. They feel unworthy. They believe they're not good enough. And they stop themselves from having the impact on the world they're meant to have.

> *It's my mission to help passionate entrepreneurs discover, love, and live their authentic selves, so they have the confidence to pursue their dreams and take their place in the world.*

It breaks my heart to see smart, competent women sell themselves short, beat themselves up with shame and self-doubt, and play small because they don't see themselves as the amazing masterpiece they're created to be. Women tell me over and over again that they've spent so much time taking care of other people's needs and living up to other people's expectations that they've lost sight of themselves. A client recently told me, "I'm ready to step out and be myself, but I'm not really sure who I am anymore."

Over the years, I've realized that it's my gift to help women uncover the layers of muck and junk that have covered up their unique

4

masterpiece, damaged their self-esteem, and hidden their greatness from the world – and themselves. It's my mission to help women discover, love and live their authentic selves, so they have the confidence to pursue their dreams and take their place in the world. So they can, like Steve Jobs said, make a dent in the universe.

Who is this book for?

This book is for you if you wish you could just get it together and be confident already. If you ever ask yourself, "Who am I to think I can be great?" this book is for you.

If your knees knock when it comes to networking, if you shake in your stilettos the minute you have to ask for the sale, you're in the right place. If you've let opportunities pass you by, if you've failed to follow up, or if you haven't pursued your dreams because you were too chicken to go for it, this is for you.

This book is for you if you've ever thought, "If I'm really called to do this, shouldn't I just serve, and not sell?" Ever been guilty of giving away the farm or charging way too little for your work?

If you have big dreams for your life and business, but secretly doubt that you're worth it, you're in the right place.

This is even for you if you've achieved success and done some big things, but you're afraid that one day you'll be "found out" an exposed as a fraud. I hear this one a *lot*, from very successful, very qualified women. If that's you, keep reading!

And finally, if you've forgotten who you are or wondered why everyone else seems so confident while you feel like a train wreck, you're totally in the right place.

> *Your self-worth either supports or sabotages your success.*

What You'll Discover

In this book, you're going to discover how your self-esteem may be holding you back from being and doing all that you were created for. Because your self-worth either supports or sabotages your success. And for most women, unfortunately, it's usually sabotage.

We'll talk about how women sabotage themselves from having the success that they want, from having the impact they're made to have. And we'll talk about how to stop the self-sabotage and step into your dreams and build a life and business you love. In short, how to know your self-worth so you can grow your net worth.

What is Self-Worth?

Self-worth is called many things. Confidence. Self-esteem. Loving yourself. Self-image. Self-concept.

First of all, I think it's important to talk about what self-worth is *not*.

It's not the false sense of self-esteem peddled by our modern society which coddles people and makes them feel entitled

> *It's the struggle, the overcoming, the getting back up after you fall that builds real self-esteem, not constant compliments and over-protection.*

just for existing. You know what I'm talking about: kids' baseball teams where everyone receives a trophy just for showing up; soccer leagues where no one keeps score so there arc no winners and losers, so as not to crush the kids' supposedly fragile self-esteem; helicopter parenting where we rescue kids from the consequences of their mistakes because we're so afraid to let them fail, lest it shatter their self-worth.

There's no foundation to that "self-esteem." That's simply an entitlement mentality that teaches people that the world *owes* them something. We do our kids a grave disservice when we don't let them struggle and fail and learn from their mistakes. It's the struggle, the overcoming, the getting back up after you fall that builds real self-esteem, not the constant compliments and over-protection.

Self-esteem also is not the attitude that "I know I'm great, and no one can tell me I'm not." One of my guilty pleasures is watching a few select reality TV shows like Project Runway. I've noticed a disturbing trend among the younger competitors in these shows. They'll be given constructive feedback from the judges, or maybe even eliminated, and they rant and rave on the exit interviews about how awesome they are, and if the judges can't see that, then that's too bad for them.

That's not self-esteem either. That's arrogance, maybe. But not self-esteem. I think it's a result of the way our society seeks to build self-esteem in people these days, by hyping them up with compliments rather than building them up with character.

Which brings me to what self-worth *is*.

> *Self-worth is about being empowered, not entitled.*

Self-worth *is* about being empowered, not entitled. It comes from knowing who you are and

8

what you were put here on this earth to do. It starts with knowing that you're an amazing masterpiece, created for greatness. But it's much more than that.

It's also founded on what I call the 3 Pillars of Self-Worth: Competence, Character, and Core Values.

The 3 Pillars of Self-Worth

Competence

The First Pillar of Sclf-Worth is Competence. Knowing that you are capable. Owning your skills and talents. Reaching for goals.

When we give kids a trophy just for showing up for practice, we teach them that hard work isn't important, only making an appearance. That doesn't build self-esteem. Working toward your goals does.

When I was in college, I trained in Tae-Kwon Do. I entered a competition in New York City with some other people from my dojo. I won my division, beating out a good friend. I got a trophy for winning. Everyone one else got a patch for participating.

Did my friend's self-esteem suffer because she didn't get a trophy just for showing up? No. In fact, that would have been insulting. After all, what's the incentive for working *at all*, let alone doing your best, if you get a trophy just for entering the arena? That trophy would have been meaningless.

Actually, as I was recalling this story, I originally thought that *my friend* had won the competition. It wasn't until I dug up a picture of our group and saw it was *me* holding the trophy that I remembered that I was the winner.

Yes, the trophy had meaning for me at the time. But what has meaning for me *now*, so many years later, is the effort I put forth, knowing I did my best and stretched myself beyond what I thought I could do. It wasn't the outcome. It was the effort.

One of the biggest problems with never letting kids fail is that they never gain real competence. See, you have to fall on your face a few times and get back up and try again.

I didn't start out being a multi-state Tae-Kwon Do champion. I fell on my butt a lot. I got bruised a lot. I failed a lot. But I kept practicing. It took years of hard work to get that good. I gained competence through failure and continued effort.

I'm sure you've experienced failure and disappointment in your business. All of us, at some point in time, have had a big sale fall through, an important client quit, or even a business just go belly-up on us.

> Competence is knowing that you can take on a challenge and come out standing.

But you don't quit. You get back up, learn your lessons – hopefully – and try again. And you do things better the next time around.

Competence isn't about never failing. It isn't about knowing how to run Facebook ads or being a copywriting genius. And it isn't about having a resume of grand, earth-shattering achievements.

It's knowing that you have the ability to figure things out, or to hire someone who can do them for you. Competence is knowing that you can learn what you need to, when you need to. It's knowing that you can take on a challenge and come out standing. It's having the perserverance to not quit when things get hard.

Character

The Second Pillar of Self-Worth is character. You feel better about yourself when you're living with integrity, when you do what's right. You've heard the phrase, "Bad company corrupts good character." Well, bad character corrupts good self-esteem.

> *Bad character corrupts good self-esteem. If you do crappy things, you'll feel crappy about yourself. It's called a conscience, and it's a good thing.*

One of my favorite movie scenes is from the Adam Sandler film "Spanglish." The main characters' marriage is on the rocks, and his wife, Deborah, decides to have an affair. One night, when she's sneaking out to meet the man, her mother confronts her. Deborah blames her mother for making her feel terrible about herself – again. Her mother stops her and says, "Right now your low self-esteem is just good common sense."

You see, she felt bad about herself, and she wanted to blame other people. But at that moment, it was her bad decisions – her character – that were contributing to her lack of self-worth.

Clearly, our self-worth often suffers because of things done to us that are beyond our control. But our actions definitely contribute to our self-esteem as well.

Let's face it: if you do crappy things, you're going to feel crappy about yourself. That's called a conscience, and it's a good thing.

Solid, unshakable self-esteem is built on living a life of integrity and good character. For kids, it's built on knowing that they tried their best in the soccer league, not that they got a trophy for simply not quitting half-way through the season. As an entrepreneur, self-esteem is built on the character you show in your business – treating clients fairly, delivering on your promises, adhering to ethical business practices.

Core Values

Closely related to character is Core Values, which is the Third Pillar of Self-Worth. Core Values are the deeply held principles and

> *When your life and decisions are in line with your core values, you feel better about yourself because you're being true to yourself.*

characteristics you want people to see in you. The qualities you want to teach your children. Things likc honesty. Generosity. Creativity. A commitment to excellence. The importance of family. A belief in God.

When you don't live in accordance with your core values, you're compromising and being hypocritical. That erodes self-esteem. But when your life and decisions are in line with your core values, you feel better about yourself, knowing that you're living authentically. You're being true to yourself.

When I work more closely with people, one of the things we do is uncover their core values, and identify the ways their lives reflect and conflict with those beliefs.

Nick Vujicic is a great example of core values in action. He was born without arms or legs. When he was a toddler, the "experts" told his parents that they should put him in a playgroup with other special needs children.

In his book, *Life Without Limits*, he writes:

> My parents... held on to the conviction that my life would have no limits, and they fought to keep that dream alive. My mother, bless her, made an important decision at an early stage of my life. "Nicholas, you need to play with normal children because you are normal. You just have a few bits and pieces missing, that's all," she said, setting the tone for years to come. She didn't want me to feel less than normal or restricted in any way. She didn't want me to become introverted, shy, or insecure just because I was different physically. (*Life Without Limits*, pg 41).

14

This early example of his parents living and making decisions based on their core values significantly influenced Nick and his self-esteem. It enabled him to live by his *own* core values, exemplified in his first book title, *Life Without Limits*.

He now travels the world speaking and inspiring thousands of people with a message of hope and self-acceptance. He says, "I promise you for every *disability* you have, you are blessed with enough *abilities* to overcome your challenges." (pg.12) He struggled a lot with self-esteem as a child, but after figuring out his identity and worth as God's child, he is a living example of core values in action.

The Self-Worth Solution

The Self-Worth Epidemic

Why is self-worth so important? Because it's an issue so many women face. But it's not like we go around telling everybody. After all, if you openly admit that you don't feel confident about yourself and your abilities, that would certainly have an impact on people's willingness to buy your products and services, wouldn't it?

So we put on a mask and don't let other people see our doubts and our insecurities. Half the time, we don't even admit it to ourselves. The thoughts creep into our heads when we're lying awake at night, unable to sleep, but we push them aside and try to ignore them.

But when you hide the problem, you can't deal with it. And not dealing with it affects your business, too, as we'll see soon.

The Mini-Cheese Bus

Half-way through kindergarten, I switched schools. I went from this small neighborhood school with a few hundred students to a giant magnet school that took kids from all over the city. Over 3,000 students attended this school. It had 3 wings with 4 floors in each wing. Just getting to my classroom was like walking through a maze.

Needless to say, on my first day, I was terrified. I wanted a little extra boost of confidence, so I'd planned to wear my Wonder Woman Underroos®. I mean, what girl wouldn't feel ready to take on the world – or at least a new school – channeling her inner Wonder Woman? But my mom had other ideas.

She insisted that I wear a white cotton dress, which meant I had to wear boring, non-bravery-booosting white panties. So when the school bus came, I was feeling less than confident.

To call this thing a bus was being generous. It was more like a van, with long bench seats from front to back. We called it the Mini Cheese Bus.

There were no steps to get into the van. The floor was above my waist, and I was too short to climb into it by myself. So my brother stood on the ground and lifted me up while his friend grabbed my arms from inside the bus and basically threw me onto the front bench seat. I landed like a beached whale, and my dress flipped up over my head. Suddenly, I was very glad I wasn't wearing my Wonder Woman Underroos®.

It was humiliating.

And it went on like this for weeks until I got tall enough, or strong enough, or smart enough to climb in by myself.

My mother, standing on our front steps on the opposite side of the bus, had no idea any of this was happening. From her perspective, everything was perfect. But inside, it was a train wreck.

And that can describe so many of us. We can seem to have it all together on the outside, but inside we're often hurting – full of self-doubt, insecurity, and a false sense of who we are. It erodes our self-esteem and keeps us from taking risks or standing out.

Your Self-Worth Affects Your Net Worth

Mika Brezezinski, co-host of MSNBC's Morning Joe, discovered that women's insecurities hold them back more than anything else when it comes to going after the success they desire. She says that "women are their own worst enemies in the workplace. I have seen time and again that we don't ask for what we're worth because we don't know or we're too scared to find out what our value is." (*Grow Your Value*, pg 19).

Even women who you'd never think in a million years would be plagued by this, experience self-doubt and a lack of love for themselves. Remember the study we talked at the beginning of the book, which showed that only 2% of women worldwide consider themselves beautiful? It may surprise you to learn who's *not* in that 2%.

> *When can seem to have it all together on the outside, but inside we're often hurting – full of self-doubt, insecurity, and a false sense of who we are.*

Jennifer Aniston, for instance, once said, "I don't feel beautiful all the time. The majority of the time I don't." When the TV show *Friends* was on the air, thousands of women flocked to salons everywhere to get her hairstyle because they wanted to look like her. It was such a phenomenon, the hairstyle became known as "The Rachel." These women thought she was beautiful enough to imitate her. Is it kind of surprising that she doesn't see herself that way?

Angelina Jolie, one of the most accomplished actors in Hollywood, once said, "I struggle with self-esteem all the time! I think everyone does. I have so much wrong with me, it's unbelievable."

It doesn't matter how rich or famous or accomplished you are. Low self-esteem doesn't discriminate. And it affects every area of a

20

woman's life. If you have low self-esteem, it's reflected in your ability to handle stress and cope with diseases like cancer and heart disease. It's been shown to contribute to mental health issues like anxiety and eating disorders. And if you're an entrepreneur, it definitely affects your business.

Think about it. How many times do you have to network? To launch a new program or take a big risk? To meet clients for the first time? To ask for the sale?

Do you feel confident in these tasks? Do you feel worthy enough to stand up for yourself and confront a client or vendor who's

> *It doesn't matter how rich or famous or accomplished you are. Low self-esteem doesn't discriminate.*

taking advantage of you, or do you blow it off and ignore it, hoping it will go away? Do you believe in yourself enough to take imperfect action in a new direction – even if it means you may be a little over your head at first – knowing you can jump in and figure things out as you go?

Or do you doubt yourself? Do you feel unworthy? Do you *know* that you could have such a greater impact if you'd just feel confident about yourself and your abilities?

There's an epidemic of low self-esteem in our world today, especially among women. And when you don't feel worthy, you sabotage yourself and your success. Let's look at some of the ways that women sabotage themselves, and why. As we go through them, think about which one – or which *ones* – you identify with.

The Self-Hater Syndrome

The first way women sabotage themselves is with The Self-Hater Syndrome. In this syndrome, you want to love yourself, but it feels selfish, so you end up tearing yourself down instead. How do you know if you're a victim of the Self-Hater Syndrome? See if you recognize yourself in any of these symptoms.

The Symptoms

You happily buy your kids everything they need (and lots of things they *don't* need), **but you hesitate to invest in your business.** Or even get a pedicure.

> *The Self-Hater: You want to love yourself, but it feels selfish, so tear yourself down instead.*

Your inner talk is a constant barrage of self-criticism. (You know, you say things to yourself that you'd never dare say to someone else.)

You feel shame about your past and you just can't seem to move past it. One of my clients had been molested for years as a child. In an effort to control her situation, she decided that she'd become so heavy that no one could ever physically force her to do anything against her will. As an adult, she weighed over 300 pounds. Not only did she carry around the shame of her past, but also the shame of her current physical appearance, poor health, and insecurity.

It wasn't until she let go of that shame and learned to love and accept herself for who she was that she was able to shed some of the weight and move on with her life. She's now 100 pounds lighter, happily married, and pursuing her dream as an English teacher and missionary overseas.

You beat yourself up when you make a mistake and have a hard time letting it go. You take every mistake as "evidence" of your incompetence, your unworthiness – or whatever negative ways you describe yourself.

You blame yourself for everything, taking responsibility even when it's not yours to take. If you work with a team, or virtual assistants, and they don't do what they're supposed to do, instead of letting them take responsibility for their actions, you immediately assume that you're at fault. You think, "Since I always screw things up, I must have done something to cause this, too."

There's a big difference between taking responsibility for your own life, your actions and decisions – which *improves* your self-esteem – and automatically assuming you're at fault and taking the blame when it's not yours to take. That sabotages self-esteem. You know, you can lead a horse to water but *don't'* feel guilty if it doesn't drink.

You're constantly comparing yourself to other people, and seeing all the ways you don't "measure up." Whether it's Pinterest, Facebook, or your professional competition, you're not content with your skills, abilities, or success because there's always someone doing better than you are.

You have big goals for your business, but secretly doubt if you're worthy of achieving them. I've been involved with various network marketing companies over the last 12 years. I'm still involved with 2 of them – one being Mary Kay cosmetics. Years ago, when I really struggled with my self-esteem, I put off joining the company because I didn't feel beautiful enough to be an Independent Beauty Consultant. After all, don't you have to be *beautiful* to be a Beauty Consultant?

I finally got over myself enough to give it a try. I soon wanted to move up in the company, grow my team and become a director – one of the top positions. But I didn't feel worthy of that achievement. I sabotaged myself with negative self-talk. My lack of self-worth significantly impacted my net worth, because I held myself back from growing my team and my customer base.

Eventually, by implementing some of the practices that I coach clients on today, I improved my self-esteem, grew my business, and moved into the top 5% of the company.

But I can't tell you the number of women I come across today who have the same insecurities I did. It breaks my heart to see them not fulfilling their dreams because they don't feel worthy, and sabotaging themselves with self-hate.

The Causes

So why do women sabotage themselves with The Self-Hater Syndrome?

I find that women, especially, believe that it's selfish to love themselves. We're told to consider others better than ourselves, to not think of ourselves more highly than we ought. If we openly express our love and acceptance for ourselves, we're called all sorts of names:

- Diva
- Bitchy
- High-maintenance
- Self-absorbed
- Stuck up

- Fake
- Conceited
- Self-centered

The list goes on.

So we become overly-critical of ourselves in an attempt to not be prideful. In an effort to appear humble, we put ourselves down and focus on our flaws. For many women I've coached, it's freeing to learn how to love themselves, and that they can do so without being arrogant.

Another reason women sabotage themselves with self-hate is that we're constantly competing with each other. We're always comparing ourselves to other women. Think about fashion and celebrity magazines. They routinely run features like, "Who Wore it Best?" where they compare two women wearing the same outfit, to see who looked better. I'm sorry, but who freaking cares?

Sure, these articles are popular and (mildly) entertaining. But they cause women to make unhealthy comparisons that ultimately lead to them feeling bad about themselves. Because there's always someone who looks better. There's always someone who's more successful.

> *We become overly critical of ourselves in an attempt to not be prideful. In an effort to appear humble, we put ourselves down and focus on our flaws.*

And this attitude can transfer over to your business. It's good to analyze your competition's marketing strategy, for instance, to see how you can improve your own efforts. It's *not* healthy to obsess over who has more clients, more revenue, or better reviews.

If you "beat" her, you might temporarily feel better about yourself. If you don't beat her, it becomes more evidence of how you don't measure up.

Either way, you let your self-worth be determined by external factors – by what you *do*, rather than who you *are*.

And while we're on the subject of comparisons, we have to talk about social media. It can have a big negative influence on the way you see yourself. You look at the perfect Pinterest craft and wonder what's wrong with you, because your version would look like a first grader did it. Or you see your friends' Facebook posts and wonder why your life isn't nearly as exciting. Numerous studies have shown a relationship between use of social media and low self-esteem.

It's been said that comparison is the enemy of contentment. If you're not careful, browsing Pinterest for some inspiration or trolling Facebook to catch up with friends can easily turn into a damaging comparison game.

And then there's advertising, in its various forms. Watch too many commercials, and we basically believe that we *can't* love ourselves because we're never beautiful enough, successful enough, or good enough without the right car, the right clothes, or the right cereal.

By trying to keep up with the Joneses and other types of unhealthy competition, we tell ourselves that we're not good enough, not smart enough, not competent enough.

> *If you're not careful, browsing Pinterest for creative inspiration or trolling Facebook to catch up with friends can easily turn into a dangerous comparison game.*

The Cure

The cure for The Self-Hater Syndrome is simple. Not necessarily easy, but simple. You need to give yourself permission to take back your power, to step into the greatness you were created for, and to love yourself unconditionally.

I'm sure you've heard the sayings, "Love your neighbor as yourself" and "Treat others the way you want to be treated." Right? It's the Golden Rule.

We all get the love your neighbor part. But the part we often miss is what's implied in that statement: We have to love *ourselves,* too.

On the one hand, the way we treat others is often a reflection of the way we feel about ourselves. If you're constantly finding fault in everyone around you, chances are you're an expert in finding your own flaws as well.

On the other hand, we often treat others better than we treat ourselves, don't we?

Think about it. What would you say to your friend who told you she's burned out with trying to balance her family life with her business life, desperate for a good night's sleep, and wanting to quit? Would you tell her to suck it up and get over herself, because that's what she signed up for when she started her business?

> Give yourself permission to take back your power, to step into the greatness you were created for, and to love yourself unconditionally.

Of course not. You'd tell her to cut herself some slack, maybe get a massage, and take a little time off with her family.

But do you practice what you preach? How often do you get too little sleep, take too little time off, and generally don't take care of yourself as well as you should?

And how often do you criticize yourself in a way you'd *never* do to someone else? We all have this voice inside our heads – I call her your Inner Mean Girl. She's the one who lies to you, accuses you, throws all your faults and failures in your face. Think about what your Inner Mean Girl tells you. Think about the things you tell yourself when you're alone. When you fail. When you're lying in bed trying to fall asleep. Be honest. What are the meanest things you say to yourself?

> *Your inner self-talk can either support you or sabotage you, breathe life into you or kill you emotionally.*

Now think about your best friend and imagine saying those things to her. Imagine telling her, "You big, fat, stupid, ugly cow. You never do anything right!"

You wouldn't say that to her, would you? Of course not, because it's mean and it's wrong. But how often do you say it to yourself?

Do you focus on all the things that are wrong with you, on all the things you don't do right? Or do you focus on everything that's good about you? In order to cure the Self-Hater Syndrome, you have to change your self-talk.

There's a Hebrew proverb that says, "Life and death are in the power of the tongue." Your words, your inner self-talk, can either support you or sabotage you, breathe life into you or kill you emotionally.

I help women speak life to themselves, to love themselves with their words as well as their actions. I help them turn that Inner Mean Girl into their Inner Mentor – their cheerleader instead of their tormentor. I help them speak truth to themselves, to speak goodness and grace to themselves. To treat themselves with the same love and respect they give *other* people they love.

It's not selfish to love yourself. It's essential.

To cure the Self-Hater Syndrome, you've also got to run your own race. Stop constantly comparing yourself to other people, and measuring your worth

> *It's not selfish to love yourself. It's essential.*

and success against theirs.

Stop taking Facebook at face value. It's so easy to make assumptions off what we see in our newsfeed, isn't it?

I think we've all got at least one friend on Facebook whose life seems beyond perfect. I've got a friend who I swear has a professional photographer follow her around all day. She's constantly posting glamorous photos of exotic vacations, girls' nights out, and photo shoots just for the heck of it – even pictures of her doing archery in 6-inch stilettos!

If I just looked at her Facebook posts, it'd be so easy to be jealous of her perfect life. But knowing her "in real life," I also know her struggles and her fears. She's an amazing woman with a great life. But it's not all target practice and awesome shoes.

And that's the downside of social media. People often post trips about their fabulous vacations, but they don't usually post about the fight they had with their husband on the way to the airport. And if they *do* post negative stuff too often, you probably unfollow them because you don't want to see the drama, right?

Author Shauna Neiquist describes Facebook as a "highlight reel" of people's lives. I think of it as a movie trailer. All the

> *You can't compare your everyday life to someone else's movie trailer, and forget that there's a ton of crappy footage on the cutting room floor.*

best scenes, none of the "filler." If you take it at face value, you can easily feel like you don't measure up. But you can't compare your everyday life to someone else's movie trailer. Those studies about depression and social media I mentioned earlier? It's because we see all the *highlights* of their life's movie and forget that there's a ton of crappy footage on the cutting-room floor.

In order to cure the Self-Hater Syndrome, you've got to run your own race, and stop comparing yourself to others.

Think about an Olympic sprinter. I'm sure she's aware of her competitors. But she's certainly not picking apart their stride in the middle of a race. She's focused on *her* stride, *her* rhythm, *her* race. To embrace your own worth, you have to focus on running your own race and stop comparing yourself to others. Stop thinking about how you don't measure up. Start focusing on *your* journey and *your* strengths. Accept yourself for who you are.

You were created as a masterpiece, and you are worthy, just as you are. When you find contentment in your own life, when you see the beauty that's inside you and the blessings that surround you, you'll feel better about yourself and gain confidence.

The Fraud Syndrome

The next way I see many mission-centered entrepreneurs sabotage themselves is with The Fraud Syndrome. This is where you're successful in your life and your business, but you're afraid you'll be "found out" and exposed as a fraud.

The Symptoms

You think, "I don't really know what I'm doing." "I'm not really qualified for this," or "if only people knew the truth."

You assume everyone else knows more than you. You're afraid to claim your expertise in an area because you're afraid to be wrong, or you're afraid you don't really know as much as you

> *The Fraud: You're successful in life and business, but you're afraid you'll be "found out" and exposed as a fraud.*

think you do. So you defer to others' opinions.

You're an overachiever or a perfectionist. Maybe you obsess over the details, working harder than anyone else. You hope somehow to "pull it off," that your effort will make up for your lack of real talent.

You remember every failure and criticism you've ever received, but you forget – or you discount – the successes and the praise. Boy, the Inner Mean Girl really works overtime in The Fraud Syndrome. You may dwell on your failures and wonder how you ever managed to have the success you do, given all the failures you've had. You internalize criticisms and believe them to be true.

But how do you handle a compliment? Do you accept it graciously, or do you deflect it, minimize it, and say to yourself, "Oh, they're just being nice?" The more praise you get – especially if you're an overachiever or perfectionist – the more it perpetuates the feeling of being a fraud and the fear of being "found out."

You worry, "What if they find out I'm just me?" Because being "just you" doesn't seem good enough.

The Causes

There are many causes of The Fraud Syndrome. I'll describe a few of them here.

It often stems from a mistaken belief that you're not really "worth it." If someone thinks you are, you must have deceived them; therefore, you're a fraud.

Sometimes it comes from comparing yourself to other people. "Well, I'm no so-and-so, I'm not the best

> Sometimes feeling like a fraud comes from believing the Myth of Perfection.

or the most famous or the most successful. I don't have this person's credentials or that degree. So I must not know what I'm talking about. I must not have *anything* to offer the world."

People with low self-esteem – and victims of The Fraud Syndrome especially – tend to internalize their failures while externalizing their successes. What I mean is this: A confident person sees their success as a result of their efforts and abilities. They have a hand in their own success. Their failures, on the other hand, are often seen as a result of poor timing, bad luck, or simply, "I'll do better next time."

But a person with low self-worth, a person who feels like a fraud, does just the opposite. They see every failure as proof that they're not "worth it," and every success as the result of mere good luck and circumstances.

Sometimes feeling like a fraud comes from believing the Myth of Perfection: if you're not perfect, you're not qualified. For example, if you're a health coach, you should never eat junk food. Or if you're a jewelry designer, you should never buy earrings from Macy's.

I was once accused of being a fraud because, even though I'm known as The Confidence Coach, I admitted to feeling fear in my business when I needed to do a whole bunch of brand-new-to-me things in a very short period of time. This woman said, "Wait, did I miss something? Didn't she say she's The Confidence Coach?"

It would have been easy to feel like a fraud after hearing that. And I admit that it did hurt my feelings for a few seconds. But then I realized that her statement was a reflection of her own misunderstanding, and the Myth of Perfection.

See, being confident and knowing your worth doesn't mean that you're never scared. In fact, as an entrepreneur, I'm sure you know that if you're never scared in your business, it means you're playing it safe and not growing. If you're pushing yourself, you're going to be scared from time to time. The difference – and what makes me qualified as The Confidence Coach – is that I've developed tricks and strategies to overcome the fear and come back to my center of confidence because I know I'm worthy. But I'm far from perfect.

Many women tell me they feel like a fraud because they're afraid to be themselves. They're afraid of rejection if they let their true selves shine through. Or they think that *have* to be like someone else to be successful.

Well let me tell you, that leads to more feelings of being a fraud. And if you're living up to someone else's expectations of you and not being true to yourself, in some ways that *is* being a fraud. Maybe you've been "in hiding" so long, you've forgotten who you really are.

If you feel like a fraud, first of all, I want you to know that you're in good company. I've read estimates that up to 70% of people *worldwide* feel like a fraud at some point in time. And it seems to affect higher achievers the most.

Even people like Seth Godin and Sonya Sotomayor have publicly admitted to feeling like a fraud. Heck, even Einstein, near

> *If you're living up to someone else's expectations of you and not being true to yourself, in some ways that **is** being a fraud.*

the end of his life, admitted to a friend, "The exaggerated esteem in which my lifework is held makes me very ill at ease. I feel compelled to think of myself as an involuntary swindler." Even *Einstein* felt like a fraud!

And the mere fact that you *feel* like a fraud is a pretty good indication that you *aren't* one. The *real* frauds are the ones who never question themselves or their motives – the ones who knowingly sell crap with a clear conscience. I know that's not you.

The Cure

One of the best ways to counteract The Fraud Syndrome is to get some perspective. See your accomplishments and talents objectively. Write them down, and for every success you've had, describe *what you did* to make it happen. Recognize that it wasn't just luck or circumstances.

> *It's helpful to look back and see the impact you're having on people's lives; it offers objective proof that you're not a fraud.*

Write down every nice thing people say about you for 2 weeks. Or 2 months. Or forever. I have a file of every thank you card, testimonial, and note of encouragement that people send me. When someone takes the time to write me and tell me how moved she was by my talk, or how she kept thinking about something I said for weeks after the fact, or how much more she loves and understands herself after working with me, I keep it. It's helpful to look back and see the impact you're having on people's lives; it offers objective proof that you're not a fraud.

The second way to cure The Fraud Syndrome is to recognize that you are enough. You. Just you. Just as you are.

Give up the Myth of Perfection. Know that your struggles make you relatable, not a hypocrite. Now, a 300-lb health coach loses some credibility. But a fit health coach who indulges in an occasional candy bar is someone who knows the value of moderation and understands the temptations of her clients.

Stop comparing yourself to others and show up in the world as your brilliant, amazing self. It may be tempting to try and be more like someone else, to imitate their style or their way of doing things. But let me tell you, if you're an entrepreneur, your customers are counting on you to be yourself.

*If you want to attract your ideal clients and build a business you love, you **must** build a brand around the Real You.*

One woman I coached was a network marketer in a party plan business. She was trying to imitate her sponsor and the way she put on parties. Well her sponsor was goofy and kind of crazy. And it totally worked for her. But when my client tried to imitate her style and her jokes, it just came off as fake, and her customers could feel it. She struggled with her sales and her recruiting efforts. But once she discovered who *she* was and honored her own unique style, her business took off.

If you want to attract your ideal clients and build a business you love, you must, must, *must* build a brand around the Real You. I love helping women discover who they are, at their core. Their core beliefs, their quirks, the unique talents they bring to the world. The world is counting on you to be you.

The Pauper Syndrome

The next way I see many mission-centered entrepreneurs sabotage themselves is by believing The Pauper Syndrome. It looks something like this: You feel guilty asking for money because you don't want to look greedy, so you give away your products or services, or grossly undervalue them. Meanwhile, you struggle to make ends meet and wonder why you're not as effective as you want to be. Maybe your clients don't get the results you know they could, and can't figure out why. It may be because you're a victim of "The Pauper Syndrome."

The Symptoms

You say things like: "If I'm really called me to do this – if I'm truly changing people's lives – shouldn't I just serve, and not sell?" Or "I really just want to make a difference. Asking for money feels icky." Or "I don't want to get rich [translation: be greedy]. I just want to help."

You don't process payments right away – or at all. I remember the first time I ever sold something from the stage. It was a workbook. The gal who bought it paid with a credit card. I couldn't process the payment on my phone, so I planned to do it later that night on my laptop. Only I never did. I put it off and put it off. It got lost under a pile on my desk. When I finally uncovered it weeks later, I decided too much time had gone by for me to process the payment without making her mad (or just embarrassing the heck out of myself). So she got a free workbook and I was out the money.

> *The Pauper: You feel guilty asking for money because you don't want to look greedy, so you undervalue your products or services.*

You give away the store (or the whole mall) because you're afraid to ask for money. That comes from having a servant's heart. But it's not a sustainable business model.

You price your products or services really low. One of my mentors calls it "trying to be the WalMart of your industry rather than the Nordstroms."

You constantly let people "pick your brain" instead of offering them the opportunity to learn it *all* (and have a bigger transformation) by investing in your product or service.

And I see this one all the time in direct sales: **You give everyone a discount** rather than expect people to pay retail.

The Causes

The causes of The Pauper Syndrome are pretty straight-forward. Somewhere along the line, many of us are taught some version of this lie: that money is the root of all evil. Actually, the *love* of money is the root of all evil, not money itself. More on that in a minute.

Maybe you were taught that money is, in essence, a zero sum game. Like the Robber Barons of the Industrial Age, people only become rich by exploiting the poor.

Or I know you've heard this one: "Money isn't everything." And it isn't. But too many women have taken it to the extreme and believe that money isn't *anything*.

I had an enlightening experience with my dad not too long ago. He asked about a 3-day event I was attending with one of my mentors. As I explained the agenda, he interrupted me and said sarcastically, "And everybody hawking their programs." Ouch. *I* sell programs.

> *Too many women have taken "Money isn't everything" to the extreme, and believe that money isn't **anything**.*

45

It dawned on me that all my life, the money story I heard was that people who sell things are charlatans and crooks. That they dupe people out of their money through manipulation and greed. That the only way people become rich is by stealing from the poor – or that if I get something, it means someone else has to go without.

It's often the most heart-centered entrepreneurs who have the hardest time asking for money. Many women ask me things like, "If people really need what I have, shouldn't I just give it to them? Why should I make them pay?"

Underneath that thought is often the underlying belief that, "My work isn't really that good." Or the fear, "What if my customers get mad at me because they didn't get their money's worth?"

Which brings me to the cure.

The Cure

Marie Forleo, entrepreneur and host of MarieTV, says that money guilt often stems from the belief that your work isn't that valuable and doesn't deserve to be sold. But if someone is willing to pay you a given amount for your work, *they* obviously believe that it's worth it. You must honor their taste and experience by accepting the money.

And the bottom line is that people pay for what they value, and they value what they pay for.

If you want true transformation in your clients, it's in *their* best interest that you charge what it's worth, and what *you're* worth.

How many "free gifts" do you have sitting on your hard drive that you've never read, or that you've totally forgotten

> *People pay for what they value, and they value what they pay for.*

about? It's the same with your clients. If you want them to be invested in their transformation, they have to be invested financially, which means you'll be compensated financially.

The more you value yourself and recognize the unique gifts you bring to the world, the more you will value the products and services you provide. And the less you'll give away for free out of fear.

One of the great things about entrepreneurs is that we really like to give, don't we? We give free content on our websites. We give free gifts to our subscribers or free samples to our customers. But at some point, you need to stop and ask for money, or you'll soon be out of business. A worker deserves his wages. And you deserve yours.

Think about it: does the electric company just give you power out of the kindness of their heart?

Hardly! They demand to be paid, and paid on time.

> *The more you value yourself and recognize the unique gifts you bring to the world, the more you will value the products and services you provide.*

We have our bill set up on auto-pay so I don't have to worry about it. Usually, we end up over-paying in the winter because it's easier to budget a consistent amount. One month, when the Phoenix heat hit early, I forgot to adjust the auto-pay amount, and I accidentally paid them $50 less than the amount due. We'd carried more than a $100 credit for months, but the *one* time we underpaid them by less than $50, we got a letter 5 days later threatening to shut off our power.

No legitimate company gives away all their services. You have no problem buying a dress at the mall and forking over the money on the price tag, even if it's a sale price or you use a coupon. You don't expect Zappos to give you a new pair of cute heels just because you want them (though wouldn't that be awesome!).

You know what they call organizations that give away their services without asking for money? Charities. And many entrepreneurs treat their business more like a charity than a business. Don't let that be you. Don't sabotage yourself with the false guilt that you shouldn't charge for your work.

The final cure for The Pauper Syndrome is realizing that money itself isn't good or bad. Remember when I said that money isn't the root of all evil, but the *love* of money is? Money is neutral. It's a tool. What matters is not how much money you make, but how you use it. Do you intend to hoard it up for yourself, or do you have bigger goals in mind with the money you want to make?

> *I never got a job from a poor person. And foundations aren't funded by people on welfare.*

I love this English proverb that says, "Money, like manure, does no good until you spread it around."

Ask yourself why you want the money. Why do you *really* want it? Like, if you were filthy rich beyond your wildest dreams, what would you do with your money?

Look, I never got a job from a poor person, and foundations aren't funded by people on welfare.

Some of the wealthiest people in the world are the biggest givers.

Oprah Winfrey has given over $400 million dollars to education projects and arts programs. Warren Buffet gave away $2.8 billion in 2014, and over $22 billion in his lifetime. That's 37% of his net worth. Bill and Melinda Gates gave $1.3 billion in 2014, and more than \$31 billion in their lifetime (41% of their net worth). They give to reform education in the U.S. and to combat diseases abroad, including the International AIDS Vaccine Initiative. (http://www.forbes.com/top-givers/)

These people aren't just making big money. They're making a big impact.

> *"Money, like manure, does no good until you spread it around."* (English Proverb)

Many people make a habit of tithing, or giving 10% of their income to churches or causes that inspire them. When you're struggling financially, you may find even a 10% tithe difficult to maintain. Imagine being able to cheerfully, eagerly give away 20, 30, even 40% of your income every year! What impact could you *really* make in this world?

So let me ask you: What's your Billion Dollar Dream? If you could solve any problem in the world, what would it be? How would

> *You making money allows abundance – freedom, life, and health – to be spread around the world.*

having millions, or even billions, of dollars to put toward that effort make a difference? What good can you do in the world if you aren't limited by money?

When you sabotage yourself with The Pauper Syndrome, you stop yourself from having a major impact on this world. You making money doesn't take it away from someone else. You making money actually allows abundance – freedom, life, and health – to be spread around the world.

The Nobody Syndrome

The final self-sabotaging syndrome I want to talk about is The Nobody Syndrome. This is where you become invisible because you don't want to look arrogant. You don't want to come across as bragging about your achievements, or appear selfish for wanting success. So you disappear and die to your dreams.

The Symptoms

You don't want to draw attention to yourself. You're afraid to speak in public. You don't stand up for yourself, rock the boat, or ask for what you want. Maybe you neglect your personal appearance, not putting in the time and effort to look your best.

> *The Nobody: You become invisible because you don't want to appear arrogant, or selfish.*

You let others take credit for your work, and your ideas.

You minimize your accomplishments. You say things like, "It was nothing," or "It's not a big deal." In her book, *Nice Girls* Still *Don't Get the Corner Office*, Lois P. Frankel tells the story of a woman whose boss complimented her for her work on a big project and gave her a bonus. The project required some very creative thinking to get the job done with a severely understaffed department.

Instead of using the opportunity to ask for a bigger team, she minimized her efforts by saying, "It really wasn't anything." Needless to say, she did not get the staff increase she so desperately needed.

You say, "Who am I to have such big dreams?" Maybe you've given up on them because they seem too lofty, or they'd put you in the spotlight.

Here's a big one that I hear from *so* many women, especially moms: **You've spent so much time taking care of other people and putting their needs above your own, that you don't know who you are anymore.** Maybe you're the proverbial Soccer Mom. Or in Arizona, where I live, it's the Baseball Mom. Your entire life and schedule revolve around your child's recreational calendar. You put your dreams on hold so that your child can pursue their interests.

If that's you, I have to ask you: have you always loved that sport, or are you defining yourself based on your *child's* activities? If so, where are *you* hiding, and when do *you* plan to come out?

You defer to other people's opinions, usually assuming that other people know more than you. This often shows up as "waffling," being unable to take a stand because each new opinion makes you change your position – again. This habit is especially dangerous for an entrepreneur, where you're called to take a stand and be a leader. It's one thing to ask for advice where appropriate, especially when it's someone else's area of expertise. But be confident enough to stand in your own expertise, go with your instincts, and be the visionary leader your customers and company need you to be.

You take a supporting role, rather than the lead. You're always in someone else's shadow. I see this a lot with direct sales consultants, again because I have a lot of experience there. Women are afraid to step up into the next level of the company because it would mean more leadership responsibilities. Or they share a meeting with someone else simply because they don't feel confident running your own meeting with their own team.

> *Be confident enough to stand in your own expertise, go with your instincts, and be the visionary leader your customers and your company need you to be.*

The Causes

There are several causes of The Nobody Syndrome. First of all, women are caretakers by nature. We know how to serve, we know how to take care of others. We're usually pretty good at it. The problem comes when your strength as a caretaker translates into guilt that you should always be giving to others, not pursuing your own goals.

I read a quote once that said that moms shouldn't put their kids' dreams on hold so they can pursue their own dreams. Rather, they should put their personal dreams on hold in order to help their kids' pursue theirs.

No, no, a thousand times *NO!* There are so many problems with this philosophy I barely know where to begin.

Your job as a parent is not to sacrifice everything so your kids can pursue their dreams. Your job is to help them be independent and strong, capable of pursuing their own dreams *in their own time.* Not at your expense. You don't have to put your life or dreams on hold for them.

> *The problem comes when your strength as a caretaker translates into guilt that you should always be giving to others, not pursuing your own goals.*

The Nobody Syndrome

Your kid won't die if you miss a baseball game now and then. Come on – it's baseball. There are like a zillion games every season It's OK to drop him off once in a while and go do something for yourself.

Let's be brutally honest here for a minute. Lots of kids love baseball. But how many will grow up to even have a *shot* at the Major Leagues? Not many. The same is true for dance, soccer, and a thousand other "dreams" our kids have.

Besides, all too often, a kid's "dreams" are little more that an Interest of the Moment. Are women to put their own dreams aside so their child can pursue something he might not even be interested in the following year? Hardly.

Please hear me on this. I'm not saying to lock your kids in the basement for 10 years while you write the next great American novel. It's good and right to support your kids and help them develop their interests.

But the best way to help your children attain their goals is to let them see you pursuing and achieving your *own* dreams. You've heard the phrase "More is caught than taught." Your kids learn by the example you set.

Do you really want your daughter growing up thinking that her dreams don't matter because she'll eventually sacrifice them for the sake of her kids anyway?

But this kind of thinking pervades modern culture and leads to so much Mommy Guilt, so many broken dreams, and so many women giving in to The Nobody Syndrome. Being a caretaker does *not* mean being a martyr.

So many women that I've worked with struggle with this very thing. They tell me that they've spent so long placing everyone else's needs and wants ahead of their own that they don't even know *what* their needs are anymore. They haven't taken care of themselves, and now they're burned out. Or they believe that pursuing their own goals is selfish because they should just be serving.

> The best way to help your children attain their goals is to let them see you pursuing and achieving your own dreams.

And to be brutally honest, sometimes it's easier to focus on helping other people live their dreams than it is to face the disappointment of your own broken dreams. Or dealing with your past and your emotional baggage and all the reasons you've given up. Sometimes it's easier to just be a Nobody than a Someone-Who-Should-Have-Been-Great-But-Wasn't.

Another cause of the Nobody Syndrome is when women let other people determine their worth.

Your past comes into play here, just like it does in the Self-Hater Syndrome. Many women carry around the burdens of their past and it weighs them down. They don't know how to let it go and find their value in the present moment. Their self-esteem is determined by someone else and they forget how amazing and powerful they truly are. They become a Nobody.

Sometimes it's easier to focus on helping other people live their dreams than it is to face the disappointment of your own broken dreams.

When women work more closely with me, one of the first things we do is identify where their emotional baggage came from. When you see it objectively, you can start to understand that your past shapes you, but it doesn't have to define you.

Thirdly, women somehow think it's arrogant or boastful to acknowledge their strengths, take credit for their achievements, or to stand out and be truly awesome. So they hide, afraid to stand out. Maybe it's a fear of seeming "unladylike." You know, we're supposed to be cooperative and not competitive, so talking about our "wins" seems like bragging.

Some women tell me that they're afraid that if they stand out, they'll leave someone behind. They'll "outshine" their friends. They want to be liked. They want to fit in. They don't want to be a "target" if they step out.

So we're guilted into mediocrity under the guise of being humble, not tooting our own horn. We hear things like "Pride comes before a fall." We're told, "Don't give in to self-promotion." I actually read this on a blog not too long ago. (Sorry, chicky, but how are you ever going to be successful as an entrepreneur if you never do any self-promotion?)

Men seem to have no problem boasting about their accomplishments. They're *never* told "Don't give in to self-promotion."

> *We're guilted into mediocrity under the guise of not tooting our own horn.*

When men desire to be rich and famous, it's not a symptom of arrogance. We chalk it up to the male ego. It's expected. But somehow it feels wrong when a woman admits that she wants fame and fortune – or any kind of success. Too many women just feel lucky to have what they do and don't want to risk the luck running out by standing up and saying, "I want more," or, "I matter."

So we tell ourselves, "Who do I think I am to have big dreams? Shouldn't I just be content with what I have, and let that be good enough?"

I want to challenge that assumption and ask, "*Why?*" Why should you passively accept what comes to you, being grateful for anything you can get, and not ask for more?

The fact that you're reading this book is proof that you're not out for selfish gain. You have a desire to serve and to make a difference in the world.

It is not selfish to stand out and be awesome, to know your worth and be somebody. It's fulfilling your purpose.

The Cure

Your dreams matter. *You* matter. You were created to do great things. But you'll never accomplish them if you're stuck in The Nobody Syndrome.

To cure The Nobody Syndrome, you have to know your self-worth, and make the decision that *you matter.* You have to combat the destructive lies that

> *Too many women just feel lucky to have what they do, and don't want to risk the luck running out by standing up and saying, "I want more," or, "I matter."*

tell women it's arrogant to stand out, to want more, or to pursue their dreams.

The key is to think of yourself with sober judgment. There are two extremes to the self-evaluation coin, and neither of them is healthy. On the one side, like we saw in The Self-Hater Syndrome, you beat yourself up over all the ways you don't measure up. The other extreme is thinking you're perfect and right all the time. One is a perpetual guilt complex. The other is flat-out arrogance. Neither one is self-worth. Rather, to know your self-worth, you must have sober judgment.

Women, especially, tend to confuse self-worth with being prideful or arrogant, like if we take credit for

something we do well, it's boastful and wrong. Sober judgment begins with realizing how amazing you really are. It's honestly acknowledging your strengths *and* weaknesses. It's recognizing your accomplishments and acknowledging that you do some pretty amazing things. It's also admitting your faults - without beating yourself up over them - and accepting yourself just as you are, even as you strive to get better every day.

In her book, *Grow Your Value*, Mika Brezezinski says that women know their value when:

> they stop beating themselves up for what they believe they *haven't* pulled off perfectly and begin to recognize how much work and life experience they bring to the table every day... It's understanding at a professional and financial level that you – your career,

perspective, hard-earned lessons, and proven techniques – are greater than the sum of your parts as a working woman.... you know where – and how – you stand out in your field, and how much you should be compensated for it. (*Grow Your Value*, pg. 3).

That, very simply, is the definition of sober judgment.

Take inventory of all the things you bring to the table – personally and professionally. Own it. Embrace it. Celebrate it. When you view yourself this clearly, your self-esteem will improve, and you'll start supporting your own success rather than sabotaging it.

Secondly, don't let anyone else determine the motives of your heart, or tell you how much is enough. Don't let anyone else tell you you're being selfish for wanting to use the gifts you've been given. Don't let anyone else determine your worth, your destiny, your purpose.

> *You can either ignore your dreams and desires and die with your message still inside you, or you can embrace it, go for it, and have the impact you're meant to have.*

Whoever said that pursuing your goals and serving others had to be mutually exclusive?

Look, no business survives if it doesn't provide great value to its customers. As a heart-centered entrepreneur, that's one of your primary goals. You're in business to help others. The more successful you are, the more people you can serve. And the more people you serve, the more successful you'll be. It's an upward spiral.

You were made with a purpose. You know it. You can feel it in your bones. You can either ignore your dreams and desires and die with your message still inside you, or you can embrace

> *It's not selfish to stand out and be awesome, to know your worth and be somebody. It's fulfilling your purpose.*

it, go for it, and have the impact you were meant to have.

Standing out does not mean you diminish anyone else. Rather, it inspires others to pursue their own dreams. When you step out and lead, you set an example for others to follow.

Think about our heroes.

> *Standing out does not diminish anyone else. Rather, it inspires others to pursue their own dreams.*

Heroes aren't the ones who never make a difference. They aren't the ones who play it safe, who fade into obscurity because they're afraid to look prideful. They're the ones who take risks. The ones who aren't afraid to stand out and be awesome.

The Nobody Syndrome

What if Amelia Earhart hadn't believed in her ability to be the first woman to fly solo across the Atlantic Ocean? What if Rosa Parks was afraid of looking selfish when she refused to move to the back of the bus? What if Sally Ride was afraid of looking arrogant when she decided to be the first female American astronaut? These women, who stood out and lived out their missions, inspired millions, and paved the way for countless women who came after them.

> *If you've got a burning desire in your heart, it's your moral obligation to pursue that passion with all your heart.*

We are all given talents, and we're expected to use them. Don't waste the opportunity you've been given by being a Nobody.

If you've got a burning desire in your heart, a mission you feel you are called to fulfill, it's your moral obligation to pursue that passion with all your heart. To go out there, to stand out, and to be awesome. You owe it to the world. And you owe it to yourself.

You were born to make a difference. It doesn't matter what your business is. You don't have to cure cancer to make a difference. Your business, your mission, your dreams are given to you to help people within your own sphere of influence.

The Self-Worth Solution

There's a Hebraic concept called "tikkun olam," which means "repairing the world." It implies that humanity has a responsibility to repair our corner of the world. That's what we're called to do, using the talents we've been given.

So I ask you, how are you called to repair your corner of the world? How would the world be different if you stopped sabotaging yourself by being a Self-Hater, a Fraud, a Pauper, or a Nobody? What impact would you make if you had the confidence to own your worth and step into the greatness you were created for?

The Self-Worth Solution

What's stopping you from knowing your worth and having the confidence to take your place in the world? What's stopping you from pursuing your dreams? What's stopping you from having the impact you were *created* to have?

Do you sabotage yourself by being a Self-Hater? Feeling like a Fraud? Thinking you need to be a Pauper? Being a Nobody? If you've identified yourself in any of the self-sabotaging syndromes in this book, you're on your way to understanding what's holding you back. Putting an end to these behaviors is the first step to owning your worth and having a big impact on the world.

But the lies and mindsets that lead to self-sabotage are just one thing that erodes your self-worth.

Poor self-esteem runs deep. It took you a long time to develop your self-esteem to where it is right now, and it takes more than just one book to make lasting change.

See, you can learn a few tricks to boost your self-esteem. You can (and should) make a list of your achievements to refer to when you feel The Fraud Syndrome coming on. You can (and should) start reciting affirmations to change your self-talk. But you can't just put an affirmation band-aid on a bleeding, broken soul and expect it to heal.

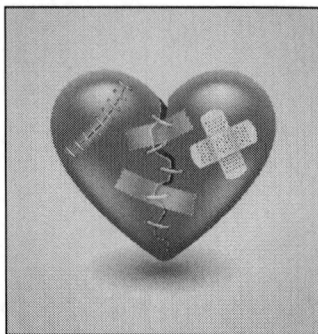

That's where too many self-improvement, self-esteem programs start and stop, and that's where my approach is different.

There's nothing wrong with affirmations. I believe in them. I use them myself, and I teach them. But you can tell yourself you're a masterpiece all day long without changing the fundamental way you see yourself. It's a true statement. But it's not enough.

> *You can't just put an affirmation band-aid on a bleeding, broken soul and expect it to heal.*

For real, lasting change to occur – to develop unshakable self-esteem and have the confidence to live your purpose – you've got to address the underlying reasons that cause you to see yourself the way you do. If you don't, you'll never have the impact that your were created to have. And you'll never have the personal, professional, and financial success that you deserve.

I've developed a comprehensive, 5-step system to know your self-worth so you can grow your self-worth. It transforms your self-esteem from the inside out by helping you discover, love, and live your authentic self so you have the confidence to live your purpose. The first step is to **Wipe Out Self-Sabotage**, which we've already addressed in depth. Step 2 is to **Outwit Spiritual Identity Thieves**.

> *A sculpture starts out as a solid block of marble, and the sculptor has to chip away all the bits and pieces that don't belong. It's the same with you.*

You are a masterpiece. You're like a beautiful, marble sculpture – hand-carved, unique, perfect. A sculpture starts out as a solid block of marble, and the sculptor has to chip away all the parts that don't belong. Michelangelo didn't build the David from the base up. He revealed it by chipping away all the bits and pieces that didn't belong.

It's the same with you. There have been experiences in your life that have hidden your masterpiece from the world – and from yourself. Experiences that made you feel Less Than. Less than worthy. Less than loveable. Less than enough. These experiences cover up your masterpiece, like the excess marble that once surrounded the David.

Maybe you hear someone's voice in your head saying you'll never amount to anything. Maybe you've had a big personal or business failure that you just can't seem to get past, and now you're gun shy about taking risks again. Maybe you were abused or had an alcoholic parent, and it changed the fundamental way you see yourself.

When things like that happen, you put up defensive walls to protect yourself from getting

> *Instead of wrecking your bank account, Spiritual Identity Thieves™ destroy your net worth.*

hurt again. Instead of feeling like a beautiful masterpiece, you feel like a clunky block of marble.

I call these experiences Spiritual Identity Thieves™. Instead of wrecking your bank account, Spiritual Identity Thieves™ destroy your self-worth. You come to believe the lies and don't see yourself clearly anymore.

I've identified six main Spiritual Identity Thieves™ that can affect the way women see themselves. They are:

1. Performance
2. The Expectations and Opinions of Others
3. Comparisons
4. Health and Reproductive Issues

5. Family

6. Abusive/Dysfunctional Relationships

When I work more closely with clients, we delve into each of these Spiritual Identity Thieves™. When they understand how their past has shaped the way they see themselves today, they're able to chip away at all the bits and pieces that aren't really them, and see their true masterpiece again.

Like Michelangelo once said, "I saw the angel in the marble and I carved until I set him free." You have to set your masterpiece free by releasing yourself from your past – from all the ways you've falsely defined yourself.

> *You have to set your masterpiece free by releasing yourself from the past, from all the ways you've falsely defined yourself.*

Once you're aware of how your identity has been shaped by your past, it's time for Step 3, **Reframe the Past**. You need to release the shame, the guilt, and the hurt feelings – to make peace with your past so you can leave it in the past where it belongs. Your past shapes you, but it doesn't have to define you.

When I work more closely with clients, we use several different techniques to accomplish this step. One tool I highly recommend is using essential oils. We use them to release fear, trauma and other negative emotions. Being trained as a scientist, I was highly skeptical of oils – they

71

seemed completely woo-woo (yes, that's the scientific term ☺) and utterly unscientific. But the more I've researched them, the more I understand their biochemical properties and the solid science behind them. I'm amazed at how effective they are when used properly.

You have to let go of the past in order to **Turn Toward the Future**, which is Step 4. Because holding onto the past while trying to live in the present is like driving across the country by looking in the rear view mirror. You *might* get there, but it'll be really slow and you're more likely to crash than to reach your destination.

> *Holding onto the past while trying to live in the present is like driving across the country by looking in the rear view mirror.*

I can help you turn your Inner Mean Girl into your Inner Mentor who pushes you forward into your destiny. I can help you turn the pain of your past into power by recognizing how your past has shaped you in a positive way – made you stronger, more resilient, a better leader. You can own your strengths and understand how they give you the ability to pursue your dreams.

This is the time when affirmations will have the most impact on your life – after you've released all the emotional baggage and gotten yourself to a place where you'll actually *believe* the affirmations you're reciting.

The final step, Step 5, is to **Honor the Real You** – to discover exactly what your unique masterpiece looks like. To know what

> *Affirmations have the most impact after you've released all the emotional baggage so you'll actually **believe** the affirmations you're reciting.*

makes you uniquely you. Your likes and dislikes. Your dreams and passions. Your experience. Your core values. Your own, individual brilliance. Everything that makes you "You."

There are probably lots of people in this world who do what you do – on the surface. There are thousands of insurance agents. Tons of social media experts. Countless life coaches. What sets you apart from your competition? Why would people choose to do business with you rather than someone else in your field?

No one does it exactly like you. You put your unique spin on things, your own unique perspective. Hopefully you can identify – and communicate – your Unique Selling Proposition.

But let's be honest. People don't make a buying decision based on what you *do*, or even *how* you do it. Not really. Buying decisions aren't logical; they're emotional. People do business with people they know, like, and trust.

The only way to get people to know, like, and trust you is by being your authentic self. Your quirks, talents and preferences are part of what makes up your unique, personal brand. Knowing – and living – your authentic masterpiece is one thing that will help you attract your ideal clients and build a tribe of raving fans who love you for you. It helps you stand out in a crowded marketplace.

> *Knowing – and living – your authentic masterpiece helps you stand out in a crowded marketplace, attract your ideal clients, and build a tribe of raving fans who love you for **you.***

It takes some digging to discover your genuine True Self, and if you're not used to acknowledging your accomplishments or seeing the good things in yourself, it can be hard to do on your own. When I work more closely with women, I teach them seven different techniques to dig deep and discover what their unique masterpiece looks like. They rediscover forgotten passions and unused talents that help them lead a more fulfilling personal and business life.

Once you discover your unique masterpiece, you have to live it – to honor that uniqueness in a very real way.

I'm going to share with you one of my favorite strategies for honoring the things that make you unique. It's a process I call Honor Your Preferences. It's actually a secret to attracting your ideal clients and building a life and business you love. Clients tell me that this is one of the most empowering exercises they learn from working with me.

> *Honoring your preferences is a secret to attracting your ideal clients and building a business you love.*

Your preferences, quite simply, are the things you enjoy, like, and would pick if given a choice. They are big things and little things. The music you prefer listening to, the kind of coffee you like, whether you want the toilet paper roll to go from the top or the bottom: these are all things that matter. Will they end hunger or bring world peace? Of course not. But they matter to you, so they matter. And honoring these preferences is a great way to boost your self-esteem very quickly.

One way I honor my preferences is through color. My favorite color is purple. It brings me joy, and I'm on a mission to color my world purple.

I also love to drink a cup of coffee in the morning, but the only coffee mugs I owned at one point were yellow. I *hate* yellow. Some people think it's bright and cheery, but it just sets me on edge.

The Self-Worth Solution

I don't know what possessed me to buy those yellow mugs, except that they were probably cheap, and I wasn't honoring my preferences at the time

> *When you honor your preferences, you send a very powerful message to yourself that **you matter.***

So every morning I'd drink my coffee, trying to relax while staring at this awful yellow mug. It drove me nuts. As silly as it sounds, I knew I'd be much happier with a purple one.

So I began searching for a purple coffee mug. It wasn't easy to find, but on a family trip to Sea World, I hit pay dirt. You see, the other thing I love, love, *love* in this world is penguins. (Don't ask me why - they're not even purple! But I'd probably own one if I could.) So coming out of the penguin exhibit in Sea World, of course I drooled over everything in the gift shop. And wouldn't you know it, I found the most perfect coffee mug in the entire world.

Because not only is it purple, it has penguins on it, too!

Needless to say, I now smile every morning when I drink my coffee from a mug I absolutely adore.

You see, it's something really insignificant in the grand scheme of things. But it brings me joy.

Your opinions and preferences really do matter, and honoring them really does make a difference. When you honor your preferences, you send a very powerful message to yourself that *you are important.*

I challenge you to find simple ways to honor your preferences in your everyday life. Incorporate some of those things into your routine. Do

> *Honoring your preferences does not mean being selfish and insisting on your way all the time. It **does** mean remembering that your wants and needs are just as important as everyone else's.*

something nice for yourself each day – even if it's simply using a yummy-scented lotion that makes you happy. If a colleague asks where you'd like to go for lunch, pick a place. If you're given a choice of which color pen to use, act like you care and pick one.

It may be uncomfortable at first. But you are worthy of getting what you want. Honoring your preferences does *not* mean being selfish and insisting on your way all the time. It *does* mean remembering that your wants and needs are just as important as everyone else's.

Because when you honor yourself in the small things, it becomes easier to honor yourself in the bigger things. The more you get in touch with the things you really desire (and, just as importantly, what you *don't* want) when it comes to "insignificant" things, the more clarity you'll have about the things that really matter.

Ask yourself if your business is filled with people you love to work with, or if you've got a bunch of pain-in-the-butt clients that drain your energy and make your business a chore. If that's the case, I challenge you to look at the way you honor your preferences in the little things.

If you're not honoring your preferences in the little things, chances are your business and your clientele reflect that.

They say that the way we do one thing is the way we do most things, right? So ask yourself if you just go through life accepting whatever's given to you, or do you make it a practice to honor your preferences throughout the day? If you're not honoring your preferences in the little things, chances are, your business and your clientele reflect that.

If you want a business filled with your ideal clients, start honoring your preferences – even in areas you think aren't related to your business. The more you get in touch with your desires in every area of your life, the sooner you'll develop a clearer understanding of who your ideal client really is. You'll start turning away non-ideal clients, or fine-tuning your marketing to attract more of your ideal ones.

Your preferences are a part of you. They're a part of your masterpiece that makes you uniquely you. They help you make your distinct fingerprint in the world.

Many of my clients say that learning to honor their preferences is one of the most significant, most empowering things they learn from the work we do together.

Try it. You'll be amazed, once you start honoring your preferences, how much your self-worth increases

.

My Gift to You

It's probably obvious that people who have good self-esteem are more likely to succeed. Most women fall prey, from time to time, to the Self-Sabotaging Syndromes described in this book. When you have poor self-worth, you may get stuck there and not know how to move past it. And if you get stuck in these behaviors for long, your business will suffer. Your light will dim and you won't have the impact on this world that you were created for. But when you have good self-esteem, you can recognize when you're sabotaging yourself and stop it in its tracks.

> *When you know your self-worth, you can grow your net worth.*

Self-worth is so much more than feeling good about yourself. It's really *knowing* yourself, and loving and accepting yourself from the inside out. You can only do that when you honestly evaluate the good, the bad, and the painful parts about yourself. You need to deal with your past and develop strategies to combat the influences –

both internal and external – that make you feel "Less Than." Only then can you see clearly enough to discover the unique, amazing masterpiece that is You.

I have a passion for supporting entrepreneurs like you. I want to help you to discover, love and live your authentic self. I want to help you know your self-worth so you can grow your net worth.

Because when you get it – when you really, truly get that you're a masterpiece, no matter how messy things may be at the moment – only then can you truly love yourself and accept yourself for who you really are. Only then can you have the courage to go after your dreams.

When you know your self-worth, you have the confidence to grow your net worth.

I have a special gift for you as a Thank You for reading this book. It's an opportunity to have a private, one-on-one Self-Worth Discovery Session with me at no cost. This one-on-one session is a $400 value.

My main objective is to have you walk away with a clear understanding of how your self-worth affects your life and your business, and what to do about it.

Even if we never talk again, after this session you will have a very clear understanding of how your self-worth affects your business success and your bottom line. You'll know what's been standing in your way of having the impact you *know* you're meant to have in your life and your business, and the best next action to take.

To take advantage of this opportunity, just go to **www.hollydoherty.com/discover** and apply for your session.

Let me tell you who this Self-Worth Discovery Session is for. This opportunity is for you if the following statements describe you:

- I'm ready to have a frank discussion about how my self-worth is holding me back from getting everything I want out of my business.
- I'm an action taker and I'm ready to make changes.
- I'm tired of missing out on opportunities because I'm too chicken to go for it, and I'm ready to be bold and confident.
- I'm tired of being defined by other people's expectations, and I'm ready to rediscover who I really am.
- I have an "invest in myself" mindset. When I see I need help, I invest the time, energy, and money necessary to get the help I need.
- I'm excited about this gift, and I fully commit to showing up for my Discovery Session, ready to take action on the suggestions I receive.

If you know you're ready to accept this gift for yourself, go to **www.hollydoherty.com/discover** and reserve your spot.

> *If you don't understand your self-worth, nothing else matters.*

Now, you may want to talk to me, but you're just not sure. Let me assure you that if you want to know what it would look like to work with me, we can certainly discuss that on the call. However, my main objective is to have you walk away with a clear understanding of how your self-worth affects your life and your business, and to know your best next step to deal with it.

If this sounds like something you'd like to do, please go ahead and apply now. You'll be emailed shortly to schedule your session. As soon as you get the email from me, click on the link to get on my calendar. Don't feed the dog. Don't check your other email. Do not pass go. Schedule your time with me right away. Look, I have two little kids, and I know how it is to have the best of intentions to get back to something, but life gets in the way and you forget. I'd hate to see that happen to you.

Because here's the deal: it's like one client recently told me: "If you don't understand your self-worth, nothing else matters."

Have you ever invested in a course that promised to transform your business, but never looked at it? Have you completed a training but never implemented anything you learned? Or made some changes to your habits, only to settle back into old patterns of behavior soon after?

See, you can take every training out there. You can invest your life savings to take your business to the next level. But if you don't

> When you know your worth, you can change the world.

believe, deep down in your soul that you are fundamentally worthy, if you don't give yourself permission to succeed and stop the self-sabotaging behaviors that prevent you from fulfilling the mission you were put on this earth to do, all the business strategies in the world won't get you to where you want to be.

On the other hand, you can have all the success in the world and earn a million dollars a year, but if you don't feel like you deserve it, you won't be fulfilled.

If you don't understand your self-worth, nothing else matters.

If you're ready to stop playing small and really "go for it" in your business; if you're ready to put an end to the constant self-criticism and doubt that stops you from having the impact you *know* you were meant to have; if you're ready to *finally* stop sabotaging yourself, and have the confidence to tackle any challenge, pursue any dream, and have a huge impact on the world, then you owe it to yourself to give yourself this gift and schedule your free Self-Worth Discovery Session today.

A client recently told me, "I wish I'd found you 10 years ago." Don't wait another 10 years to know your self-worth. Don't wait another 10 years to love yourself and have the confidence to go after your dreams.

> If you don't believe that you are fundamentally worthy, all the business strategies in the world won't get you where you want to be.

You are a masterpiece. You were created with a purpose. Don't let insecurity and self-doubt hold you back any longer.

You have a passion – a message or service to offer the world. When you lack confidence because you don't know your worth, it dims your light and keeps you from making the impact on the world that you were born to have.

You're also leaving a legacy for those who come after you. If you have children, think about what they're learning by watching you. It's been said that "Your children will become what you are. So be what you want them to be." Do you want them to be confident enough to pursue their dreams? Well, who are they going to learn it from?

It starts with *you* knowing your worth and having the confidence to live *your* purpose.

If you don't understand your self-worth, nothing else matters. But when you know your worth, you can change the world.

> *Don't wait another ten years to have the confidence to go after your dreams.*

So go ahead, right now while you're reading this. Go to **www.hollydoherty.com/discover** and fill out your application for your one-on-one Self-Worth Discovery Session.

Go ahead.

You're worth it.

The Self-Worth Solution

About the Author

Holly Doherty, the Confidence Coach, is a speaker, author, and coach who works with passionate entrepreneurs who are tired of doubting themselves and are ready to **know their self-worth so they can grow their net worth.**

Drawing on lessons she learned from her own struggle to restore her self-esteem following more than 20 years of abuse, Holly brings a message of hope and healing that empowers women to see the connection between their self-esteem and success.

Like a modern-day Michelangelo, Holly Doherty helps women chisel away all the bits and pieces of their identity that falsely define them. She helps **them discover, love, and live their authentic selves so they have the confidence to pursue their dreams**.

She loves penguins, Latin music, and ballroom dancing. Obsessed with all things purple, she strives to move toward a more minimalist lifestyle while maintaining an epic collection of sparkly jewelry and cute shoes.

To find out more, visit www.HollyDoherty.com

Resources

Book Holly to Speak
Holly is an experienced speaker who teaches entrepreneurs to know their self-worth so they can grow their net worth. Whether it's a podcast, telesummit, or live event, Holly is known for touching women's lives with her authentic and heart-felt speaking style.
Find out more at HollyDoherty.com/speaking

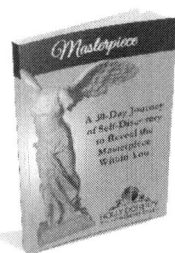

Re-discover the Real You.
This powerful course helps you release the emotional baggage that makes you feel "Less Than," and brings you face-to-face with your true, amazing self.
Find out more at HollyDoherty.com

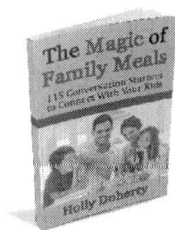

Build Your Kids' Self-Esteem.
Help your children discover their authentic selves. Re-connect with your family over a meal and watch the magic happen. Available for fundraisers.
Find out more at HollyDoherty.com/books
Also available on Amazon.

Made in the USA
San Bernardino, CA
09 April 2016